How Anyone Can Be a Millionaire in Alaska. (If They Try)

A MATHEMATICAL ADVENTURE TO FINANCIAL FREEDOM IN THE LAST FRONTIER

By: Dr. Silence DoGood

Copyrights @ 2021 by: Dr. Silence DoGood

All Rights Reserved

Dedicated To

The Holy and Great Spirit, my parents, Jim Rogers, John Rogers Jr., Fred Rogers, my students who taught me about their Yup'ik culture and all of the students who ever hated math.

Special Thanks To

Alaska Department of Revenue for making this book possible, and sharing the wealth with the Permanent Fund Dividend Division. Jack Bogle, former Alaskan Governor Jay Hammond, and the hardworking Alaskans in the oil industry. Also, for friends and family in the Armed Forces who protect our U.S. constitutional rights and interests.

Acknowledgement:

Aesop, the Tortoise, and the Hare.

Who is this book for?

Anyone who wants to learn more about Alaska's best kept secret!

Anyone who wants to be a millionaire, legally.

Especially, for my amazing students who work hard, and their current, and future families.

Who is this book not for?

Anyone who wants to get rich quick or make money illegally.

Table of Contents

Chapter 1: Why can anyone become a millionaire in Alaska faster than in other states?..1

Chapter 2: How can you become a millionaire in Alaska? 3

Chapter 3: What is the risk and what are the reasons to take the risk?..9

ABOUT THE AUTHOR 17

CHAPTER 1

WHY CAN ANYONE BECOME A MILLIONAIRE IN ALASKA FASTER THAN IN OTHER STATES?

Somewhere in the highway in the sky, Hare and Tortoise are on a plane travelling to a big race, having a stimulating conversation.

"Why can anyone become a millionaire in Alaska faster than any other states in the U.S.?" asked Hare.

"First of all, did you know that Alaska pays citizens an average of $1,000-$2,000 annually to live there if they register for the Permanent Fund Dividend?" said Tortoise.

"I get it. So, I could just save the money and over time I would become a millionaire. Thanks Tortoise!" said Hare.

How anyone can be a Millionaire in Alaska

"Not so fast Hare," said Tortoise. "It would take you approximately 500 years to become a millionaire if you saved $2,000 a year in your piggy bank."

"What about if I deposited it into a savings account at a bank or credit union?" asked Hare.

"Silly rabbit, even if you were smart and deposited that money into a savings account, where your money is insured up to $250,000, and they pay you interest, it would still take almost 500 years with interest rates at historic lows (0.01%-3%)" said Tortoise.

"Well then, how can I become a millionaire in Alaska?" asked Hare.

"You can become a millionaire in Alaska by checking your eligibility here https://pfd.alaska.gov/Eligibility, then applying for the Permanent Fund Dividend here https://pfd.alaska.gov/Application, then taking that Permanent Dividend Fund (PFD) check and investing it," said Tortoise.

"Do you know the difference between saving and investing Hare?" asked Tortoise.

"No, because no one has ever taught me," said Hare.

Chapter 2

How Can You Become a Millionaire in Alaska?

"Education is life itself. Take ownership of your life and never let your schooling interfere with your education." said Tortoise. "Both saving and investing are verbs, however, they have different purposes. Many people get them confused, so allow me to explain the difference. We save for emergencies like, injuries or health issues, car or cell phone repairs, and for big items or opportunities like a dream vacation, a concert of our favorite band, for college, or for a down payment on a new car or home. We invest to grow our money for retirement or when we no longer wish to work and have enough money to pay for our wants, needs, and taxes. We invest in assets. Assets are things that can pay us income and even grow in value over time like stocks or parts of a company, businesses, or real estate such as homes or land that we can rent to others. When we invest, we tell our money to get a job and our money works for us" said Tortoise.

"Is our money working a 9 to 5 for us, or is it working for us even when we sleep?" asked Hare.

"Yes, Hare, the money we invest is working for us even in our sleep. We call this *passive* income." said Tortoise.

"So how can I become a millionaire in Alaska?" said Hare.

"You can become a millionaire simply by taking the money the Alaskan government gives you and investing it in an index fund using a ROTH IRA. Index funds are a combination of many stocks. I will explain more later but first let me show you the money! Take a look at these graphs and ROTH IRA calculators and tell me what you see" said the Tortoise.

Dr. Silence Dogood

Graph created online at NerdWallet www.nerdwallet.com/investing/roth-ira-calculator

"I don't believe that if I invest $2,000 into the stock market that I will have $1,000,000 by age 65. Sorry Tortoise, the graph shows an error message and I'm not buying it." said Hare.

"That's understandable, Hare. You are being healthily skeptical like a doctor. Take a look at this calculator from AARP showing what would happen if you invested $2,000 each year from age 15 to age 67" said Tortoise.

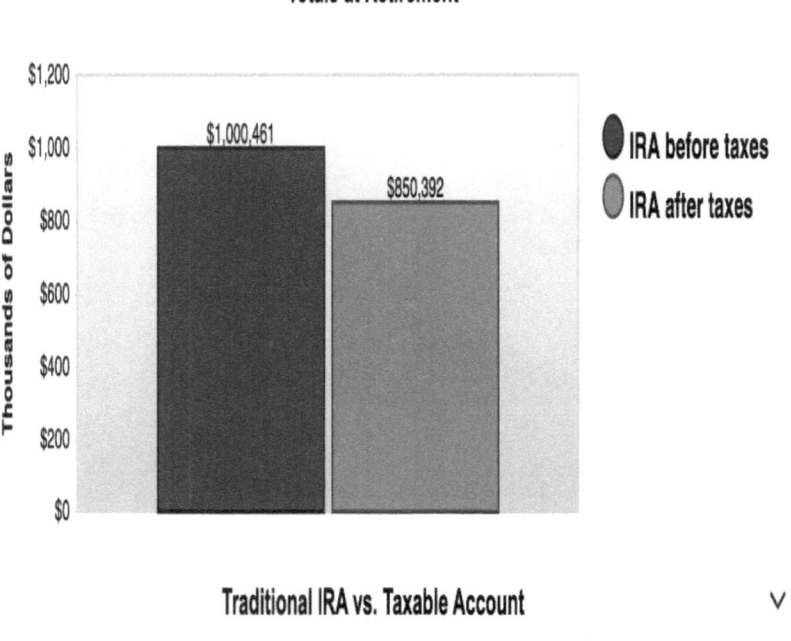

"I'm sorry, Tortoise. I am younger than 15 and would not like to retire at age 67, as I would be too old. I'd rather spend it and enjoy life more while I'm young. YOLO!" said Hare.

"It is your life and your money, Hare. Time is not money, time is life. You have the freedom to spend both how you like. However, couldn't you still live an amazing life spending money you earn from work and invest the money you receive from the Permanent Fund Dividend Division of the Alaska Dept. of Revenue? By doing this you can not only live *YOLO* now, but you can also have financial security to live *YOLO* later. Now, can you spot the differences between these graphs?" said Tortoise.

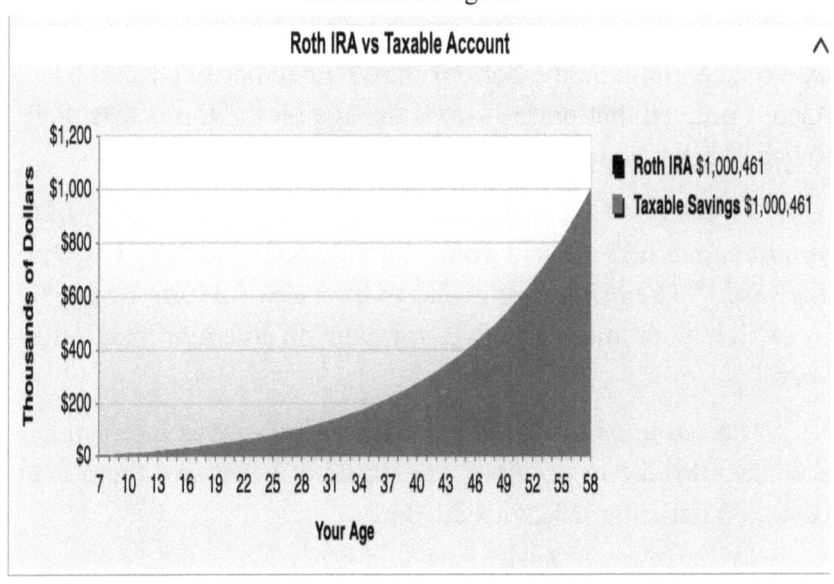

Graph created online at Thrivent www.thrivent.com/tools/calculators/roth-ira.html

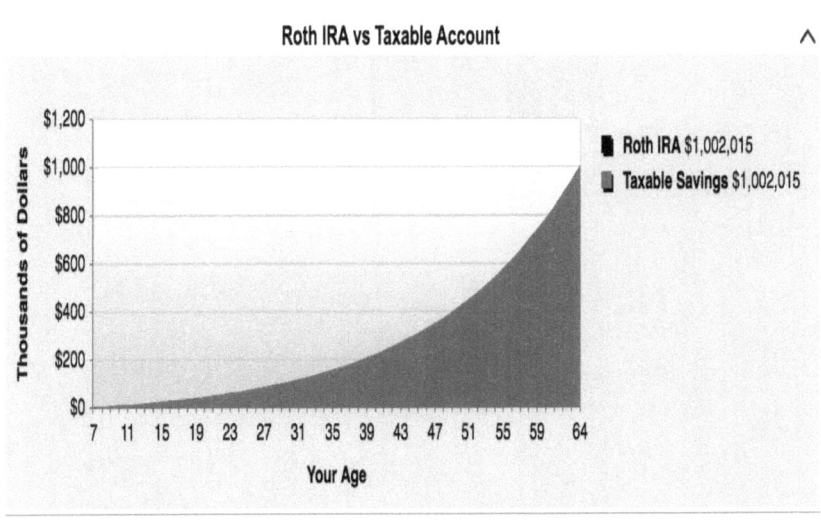

Graph created online at Thrivent https://www.thrivent.com/tools/calculators/roth-ira.html

"Yes, the y-axis on top has a balance of $1,000,461, and y-axis on the graph on the bottom shows a balance of $1,002,015. Also, I noticed that on the x-axis the age on the top is less than the age on the bottom. I wonder why that is?" said Hare.

"Great question, and good analysis Hare. It sounds like you have learned a lot in your math classes with Mr. T." said Tortoise. "The difference is due to the rate of return, or the % by which your money grows for you on average year after year."

"This sounds too good to be true. I mean it is interesting, and I would like to do more research, but I feel like there is a catch. What's the risk?" asked Hare.

CHAPTER 3

WHAT IS THE RISK AND WHAT ARE THE REASONS TO TAKE THE RISK?

"Good question. Investing your money always carries the risk of loss Hare. Before you invest, it is important to open the right account that will save you the most money" said Tortoise. "I would suggest you research the ROTH IRA, which is a gift from the U.S. government because it allows your money to grow tax free.

I=individual R=retirement A=account."

"ROTH IRA...got it. Actually, hold it right there, Mister Tortoise and let me write all of this down" said Hare.

"Smart choice, Hare. I hear, I forget. I see, I remember. I do, I understand" said Tortoise. "If you are under the age of 18, you will need a parent or guardian to help you open a custodial ROTH IRA. You can try Charles Schwab, Vanguard, E-trade, Ameritrade, Fidelity, or any other company you like. Some companies may even give you money just to open a ROTH IRA with them, which is nice." said Tortoise.

"Once you open the account, you could invest in what are called index funds, which is a combination of stocks and bonds that match the performance of the entire S & P 500, or top 500 companies. There are many stocks and funds you could invest in with varying fees. However, Mr. Buffett, who is one of the richest men in the world and greatest stock investors, said 'by periodically investing in an index fund, the know-nothing investors can actually outperform most investment professionals.'" said Tortoise.

"Okay, but why can't I just invest in one company, like Tesla?" said Hare.

"Have you ever heard the expression do not put all of your eggs in one basket?" asked Tortoise. Hare nodded. "Sure, you could invest in one company, and Tesla had one of the greatest years in terms of return on investment (%). In fact, investing in TSLA would have made you a lot of money this year. However, to reduce and better manage risk, it is often considered better to have many of the best performing stocks instead of than just one," said Tortoise.

"I see…" Hare pondered, "but what if the stock market goes down? Wouldn't it be better to just keep it in a savings account?" asked Hare.

"The stock market has gone down in the past, Hare, and investing always carries risk. However, some very smart people consider it riskier to not to invest because savings interest cannot grow your money fast enough. You need to think about your future, and how you will replace the money you earn at your job when are too old to work, or simply do not want to work any longer.

Let's take a look at the history of the stock market. Keep in mind the first index fund was created in 1975 by Jack Bogle for everyday Americans on main street not just on Wall street."

Dr. Silence Dogood

Resilience of the U.S. stock market
History of moving through difficult times

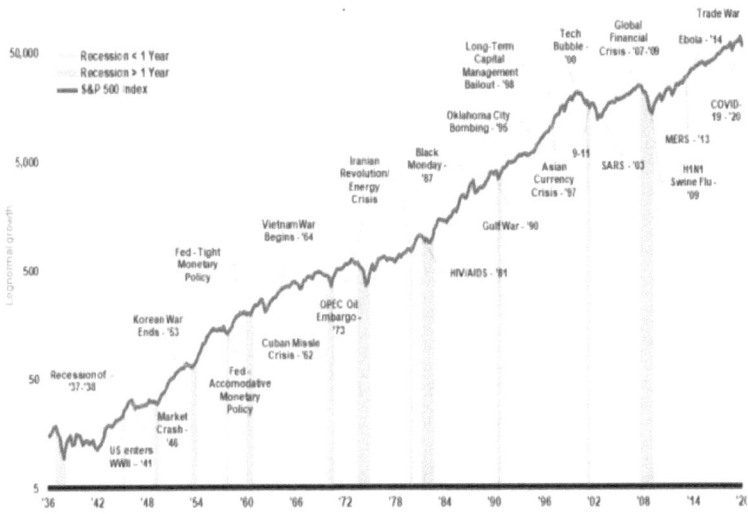

Source: Morningstar Direct – S&P 500 Index, St. Louis Federal Reserve. Data as of 3/31/2020

"Wow! So, it has gone down in the past and even crashed a few times but in the long term it has gone up." said Hare.

"Yes, many large companies have gone bankrupt in the past. Yes, there have been stock market crashes in the past. Yes, the Alaska Department of Revenue could stop sending the $1,000-$2,000 checks if the oil reserves are exhausted or they change laws even though it's coming from a *Permanent* Fund Dividend Division. All of those are real risks that must be assessed. However, investing in the market through an S&P 500 index fund offers you a higher probability that your money will grow for you in the long term. This may be the easiest route for you as a young person, however, if you are interested, you can view all asset classes and their returns over time here.

www.portfoliovisualizer.com/historical-asset-class-returns

Time and money are gifts, and you are free to do with them as you wish. But if you become a millionaire, you will not only be able to take care of yourself, but you will be able to take care of yourself so well that you will be able to take of others as well," said Tortoise.

"So, let me review my notes and make sure I was listening to you correctly Tortoise.

- **Step 1**: Check eligibility for PFD https://pfd.alaska.gov/Eligibility/Requirements, and apply here https://pfd.alaska.gov/Application.

- **Step 2:** I can take the annual check of $2,000 that the Alaska Department of Revenue sends to each of its citizens, and deposit it into a savings account at a bank or credit union.

- **Step 3**: I can open a ROTH IRA at Charles Schwab, Vanguard, Fidelity, E-trade, Ameritrade, or Betterment with my parent or guardian.

- **Step 4**: I can babysit, model, mow the lawn, lifeguard, to *earn income* to qualify to contribute to ROTH IRA. The PFD is considered *unearned income* so you will need to earn some income through self-employment or formal employment.

- **Step 5**: I can transfer the $2,000 from my savings account into my ROTH IRA account.

- **Step 6**: I can then invest in an index fund in the ROTH IRA like Vanguard 500 Index Fund, Investor Shares (VFINX), Schwab S&P 500 Index Fund (SWPPX), or Fidelity 500 Index Fund (FXAIX). I can ask my parents, grandparents, and other adults to match my contribution to make my money grow even faster for me.
  https://www.investopedia.com/can-teenagers-invest-in-roth-iras-4770663
  https://www.fidelity.com/learning-center/personal-finance/retirement/turbocharge-childs-retirement

- **Step 7**: I can live in my parents' basement and play Minecraft, and still become a millionaire with a high probability as long as the state of Alaska keeps sending me the $2,000 check, and as long as my parents don't kick me out." said Hare sarcastically.

"Yes, as long as they don't kick you out, that sounds about right. But talk is cheap, and knowledge is only power if it is applied," said Tortoise.

"Thanks" said Hare. "I think I'm going to change my habits and invest. It sounds like a lot of fun."

"To get rich and have fun…are those the only two reasons you think I shared this knowledge with you today?" asked Tortoise.

"Yes, and to take care of myself so well that I can take of others, like my family." said Hare.

"Good answer but it's much more than that. Do you know what the number one cause of stress is in the U.S.?" asked Tortoise.

"Yes, family! Or wait maybe it's work!" exclaimed Hare.

"No, Hare, the number one cause of stress and divorce in the U.S. is money, according to research by the American Psychological Association," said Tortoise. "COVID-19 has caused enough stress for 5 generations…what if we could reduce the #1 cause of stress in the U.S.?"

Hare nodded listening attentively.

"When people are stressed out, they behave differently and are often mean towards one another," said Tortoise. "How would people act towards one another if everyone didn't have to worry so much about the #1 cause of stress in the U.S.? Furthermore, did you know that stress causes health issues?

Health issues lead to hospital bills, which are the number one cause of bankruptcy in the U.S." said Tortoise.

"I didn't know that Tortoise!" said Hare.

"There is nothing funny about money if we use it wisely," said Tortoise. "Just think, Hare, what if Alaska didn't have to spend so much tax-payer money to take care of citizens through social programs? What if citizens were taking care of themselves so well, that they were able to take care of others? What could Alaska do with all of those savings? What would Alaska look like with less poverty, and more resilient families and communities? What if people didn't have to work so much, and could do more of what they love with the people they love?

"That would make Alaska an even more beautiful place." said Hare.

The plane landed.

"Now hurry up, Tortoise! We're going to be late for the Iditarod Trail Sled Dog Race.

THE END. OR

MAYBE ONLY THE BEGINNING?

This book would not be possible without Governor Jay Hammond, Jack Bogle, and hard working Alaskans. This year Alaska's Permanent Fund has a historic high value of $81.1 billion returning a strong 29.73% to Alaska as of August 3, 2021. Learn more about the history of the fund, payment history, and value below.

Check PFD Value: https://apfc.org/

Check Eligibility: https://pfd.alaska.gov/Eligibility

Apply here: https://myinfo.pfd.dor.alaska.gov/

Thank you, Governor Jay Hammond, for signing a bill in 1980 creating the Alaska Permanent Fund Corporation (APFC) for the purpose of managing investments. That year Legislature approved the first Permanent Fund Dividend program, and the first dividend check of $1,000 was distributed two years later.

Thank you and R.I.P. Jack Bogle! You changed the way we invest in the long term by inventing the index fund in 1975. You have done so much for young and old Americans and their families despite the haters. May you be remembered!

Dr. Silence Dogood
ABOUT THE AUTHOR

Dr. Silence DoGood is just a teacher certified in Math, Economics, English, and Geography who believes in you and wants you and your family to increase your wealth and reduce financial stress. He won an award from a governor in 2012 for his work in financial education and creating private public partnerships to increase financial capability among youth and adults. He wants you to enlist and invest in fighting poverty daily through financial education and strong decisive action.

How anyone can be a Millionaire in Alaska

Knowledge is power when it is applied.

Many people suffer from a lack of knowledge.

Most social problems are rooted in economic inequality and a lack of knowledge.

Can you solve this one step equation to answer the question below.

How do you empower yourself?

$$\frac{Power}{You} = Knowledge\ (\textit{information})$$

www.ingramcontent.com/pod-product-compliance
Lightning Source LLC
Chambersburg PA
CBHW031523210526
45464CB00007B/3014